IN BETWEEN

John Wedgwood Clarke was born in St Ives, Cornwall. He studied English at the University of York and lived in the city for ten years. He now works as a freelance writer and editor, and is a lecturer in Creative Writing at the University of Hull. His debut pamphlet *Sea Swim* was published by Valley Press in 2012, followed by a first full-length collection, *Ghost Pot*, in 2013.

In Between

Poems from the snickets of York

JOHN WEDGWOOD CLARKE

Valley Press

First published in 2014 by Valley Press
Woodend, The Crescent, Scarborough, YO11 2PW
www.valleypressuk.com

ISBN: 978-1-908853-41-7
Cat. no. VP0061

Cover photograph © Chris Jones 2014

A CIP record for this book is
available from the British Library

Printed and bound in Great Britain by
Imprint Digital, Upton Pyne, Exeter

www.valleypressuk.com/authors/johnwedgwoodclarke

Contents

Straker's Passage 9

Precentor's Court 10

Mad Alice Lane 11

In Banana Warehouse 12

High Petergate 13

Surveillance 14

Black Horse Passage 15

Whip ma whop ma gate 16

Lady Peckitt's Yard 17

Early Music Centre 18

Three Cranes Lane 19

Hornby's Passage 20

Unitarian Chapel 21

St. William's College 22

Holy Trinity Goodramgate 23

Barley Corn Yard 24

Starre Inn Passage 25

St Michael Le Belfry Old Hall 26

Listen to your breath as someone else.
The passage clears its throat – a winding breeze.

Straker's Passage

Tend my gutter gardens with your eyes.
Touch me up, fumble into entrances,
tag my curves, follow footfalls
to the centre of your maze.
If you span this brick with your hand,
I'll grant you it back: cobbled skin,
flakes, crust and cloth. Geese on the Foss
bray clear through the clearance
of this scum, this hole in the city,
named for the stick slid across the surface
of corn measures, removing all excess,
the spilt seed gathered up and sold.

Precentor's Court

All the bodies that have passed through here
pass through in yours, our shape
found in angles of light on a wall,
in fine hair-shadow on white render,

your passing destination a hobnailed door,
dormant house, that place where life
steps over thresholds, pausing to be led
by clouds, before re-entering the story.

Mad Alice Lane

You're between me and where I want to be.
I'm between you, walking through you,
in pigeon-clatter, drain-gurgle, vented air.
Crouch with me in the city's inner ear.
Balanced on the balls of your feet, hear your life
walk by. A pool of light, reflected
from a hidden window, comes and goes.
Do I even exist, was I hung for being
here and there? No record of me
or all the moment moving in your breath.
No price on anything, a voice complains
from the other side. Spider, the silversmith,
has rigged a wall of bricks with web.
Climb with your eyes, time's in tatters.
A man, framed by the entrance to this way,
rigid, bent, as if about to sprint, shakes his fist:
this time, this time, I'll make it through.

In Banana Warehouse

I met the second-hand past
of our first-hand love –
the Anglepoise, three oak chairs,
things behind things.

High Petergate

Feet and bikes dip in and out of puddles
drawing the city out, their trails
soft horns recoiling into pavement
as briefly as what – a slight vibration in the gutter,
water-breath, daffodils in buckets?
Ah, pedestrians and cyclists
how you waver up from the ground and open.

Surveillance

The camera's a rat in a hole
above the passage
where it threads between parking bays
and the stub-end of road.

Look it right in the eye: what a nose
it has for everything,
omnivorous, and never more
than a glance away.

Black Horse Passage

Ride the black horse of the spaces between you,
policeman, whoremaster, big man, little boy.
O Nymphs of the Pave, rain dries back to cracks.
O whores of York, where is your bricked up rage?

Here's the place to watch your step, fear the corner,
needle, junk; to cross internal borders of the city,
ancient checkpoints of flesh and soul,
where the straight line and the curved run down to water.

Whip ma whop ma gate

Walls like flat-packed history.
This is not Ikea, cut through!
It's just a joke down there, escape
into this fleshy light, airy way.

Lady Peckitt's Yard

Out of the sunshine, a place to inhale shades –
The city's revisions of breath:
Bake House, Bacusgail, Cheats Lane,
a drift mine into secrecy
now owned by no one but a name,
the cigarette's burning smeared across a stone.

Early Music Centre

Sticks blown together
under the Norman arch:
host for an eddying wind.

Three Cranes Lane

Men with keys, sticky beer, masonry,
bird shit, broken glass –
same old, same old.

And from the sewer:
lapis lazuli, counters, signet stones,
thin spoons for powders.

Hornby's Passage

Eyewash: Roman oculist *Julius Alexander's*
salve for irritations –
The back of the yard's glassed blank
by New Look, the old pillar-box blindfolded,

as if it had wandered in off Stonegate
feeling for the addresses of the dead,
their whereabouts curled in the light of old glass.

Unitarian Chapel

Light passes through one window,
spans the still interior

(wood song, fly husk, mote prayer)

catches the corner of a leaf
etched clear in red glass, shining outside.

St. William's College

Twists of light: a silver propelling pencil
beside scattered screws. Figures
ascend the East Window in a green haze
of netting, tending perpetual spring,
their hands careful with hard-won sap.
Stone shrubs, exhausted by flames
of weather, line up on the ground,
kerfs clean-cut, revealing names
as fresh as newly-split fossils.
Leaf-blower, come blow your petroleum horn.
The city grows into itself; the city
resounds like a forest, lifts us up
in its branches. Our shadows flicker
round the Minster as it sways in the light.

Holy Trinity Goodramgate

1.

Just off Low Petergate
where I bought that shirt
(blue cotton
red-thread trim)
I tried on your sarcophagus,
my head dovetailing into stone,
a perfect fit,
light as a shadow
sailing through my bones –
I wear it still,
though now it's letting in the cold.

2.

Rigged with words
and ready to cast off,

a stone boat rolls on echoes
of heavy groundswell

rising and falling
in the high-tide harbour.

And whither shall it go?
Into the scent of roses –

Barley Corn Yard

Where shops peter out into PR offices
and purchases take their toll,
a crack crawls, pageant-like, up a wall,

its tell-tales spanning the impossible
gap between a figure staring down
into the well of a screen, and a bridge

giving way, the crowds toppling into the Ouse,
St William, the cause of it all, on hand
to ensure that no one's drowned.

Show me grain heaped in the heart of the city.
A pollen-dusted car pulls into the yard.
John Barleycorn rises again as palm trees.

Starre Inn Passage

Who yaf me drynke? Life and death from a hole in the city –
Such thirst! What says the common ground,
hemmed and bounded, shit-strewn and leaky?

You're not welcome: the rivers are yours,
flavoured by your bodies; what flows from you,
returns to you: the wretched retching, retching wretched –

How the city drinks the dead down until its walls
overfloweth –

St Michael Le Belfry Old Hall

They enter, hungry, stooped, following
the old paths and rhythms of the city:
cutlery and voices from the kitchen hatchway,
alms, custard creams, *Corpus Christi* ...

Gawain, *The Book of Hours*, words like jewels
in the great halls; now ragwort proclaims
spring from the ledge of a blind window
that's wandered from its missing room.

Laughter in the common light, they pass through
in their worlds, connected by a moving
body of light, passageway of need, cleared
by a breeze from forests to the North.

Acknowledgements

Thanks are due to the University of York's YuFund for a grant that enabled the writing of some of these poems; and to Dr Kate Giles in the Archaeology Department at the University of York, who believed in the 'Past Orders' project enough to make it happen.

Some of the poems in this pamphlet were informed by research undertaken by students at the University of York, and my thanks to them for their insight and enthusiasm. Finally, I'd like to thank the curators of York Curiouser, Hazel Colquhoun and Lara Goodband for commissioning these poems, and for their understanding of the role poetry can play in a public art context.